Mary Throughout Infinity:
The Story of the Mother of God
Part 1

Rayfiel G Mychal

Copyright © 2018

DEDICATION:

This book is dedicated to Msgr. Fr. Jim C. Gehl, my mom (who is also named Mary), everybody out there with the name Mary and to the Virgin Mary. (I wonder if she will ask me for an autograph).

Table of Contents

Table of Contents iv

Before the Story 5

Part 1 7

    Origins 8

    Prophesy of the Mother of God 12

Part 2 15

    Mary's Beginning 16

    The Prophesy is Fulfilled 17

    Blessed Among Women 20

    In a Dream 22

    No Room at the Inn 23

    The Prophecy of Sorrows 25

    The Slaughter of the Innocents 26

    At My Father's House 27

    Mary the Intercessor 29

    The Sentence is Death 30

    The Way of the Cross 33

The Crucifixion 35

In the Arms of Mary 37

Farewell 38

Pentecost 39

The Queen of Heaven 40

First Church 42

Part 3 44

The Virgin Mary's First Apparition 45

Our Lady of Garabandal 46

Our Lady of Family Values 49

Our Lady of Mercy 51

Our Lady of Ocotlan 52

Our Lady of Saint-Cordon 53

Our Lady of the Fountain, Italy 54

Our Lady of the Miraculous Medal 55

The Mother of True Lights 57

Apparition to Elizabeth Canori Mora 58

Mother of the Word 59

Our Lady of EDSA 61

Our Lady of Gietrzwald 63

Our Lady of Pellevoisin 64

Our Lady of Soufanieh 65

Our Lady of Walsingham 67

Reconciler of Nations 68

Our Lady of Eternal Aid 70

Our Lady of Good Help 72

Our Lady of Good Success 73

Our Father

Our Father,
Who art in heaven,
hallowed be Thy name;
Thy kingdom come;
Thy will be done on earth as it is in heaven.
Give us this day our daily bread;
and forgive us our trespasses
as we forgive those who trespass against us;
and lead us not into temptation,
but deliver us from evil. Amen.

Hail Mary

Hail Mary, full of grace. The Lord is with thee.
Blessed art thou amongst women,
and blessed is the fruit of thy womb, Jesus.
Holy Mary, Mother of God,
pray for us sinners,
now and at the hour of our death. Amen.

Glory Be

Glory be to the Father,
and to the Son,
and to the Holy Spirit,
as it was in the beginning,
is now, and ever shall be,
world without end. Amen.

The Angelus

The Angel of the Lord declared to Mary:
And she conceived of the Holy Spirit.

Hail Mary, full of grace, the Lord is with thee; blessed art thou among women and blessed is the fruit of thy womb, Jesus. Holy Mary, Mother of God, pray for us sinners, now and at the hour of
our death. Amen.

Behold the handmaid of the Lord: Be it done unto me according to Thy word.

Hail Mary . . .

And the Word was made Flesh: And dwelt among us.

Hail Mary . . .

Pray for us, O Holy Mother of God, that we may be made worthy of the promises of Christ.

Let us pray:

Pour forth, we beseech Thee, O Lord, Thy grace into our hearts; that we, to whom the incarnation of Christ, Thy Son, was made known by the message of an angel, may by His Passion and Cross be brought to the glory of His Resurrection, through the same Christ Our Lord.

Amen.

Hail, Holy Queen

Hail, holy Queen, Mother of Mercy!

Our life, our sweetness, and our hope!
To thee do we cry, poor banished
children of Eve, to thee do we send
up our sighs, mourning and weeping
in this valley, of tears.

Turn, then, most gracious advocate,
thine eyes of mercy toward us; and
after this our exile show unto us the
blessed fruit of thy womb Jesus;
O clement, O loving, O sweet virgin Mary.

Pray for us, O holy Mother of God

That we may be made worthy of the
promises of Christ.

Amen

The Canticle of Mary

And Mary said:

"My soul proclaims the greatness of the Lord;
my spirit rejoices in God my savior.
For he has looked upon his handmaid's lowliness;
behold, from now on will all ages call me blessed.
The Mighty One has done great things for me,
and holy is his name.
His mercy is from age to age
to those who fear him.
He has shown might with his arm,
dispersed the arrogant of mind and heart.
He has thrown down the rulers from their thrones
but lifted up the lowly.
The hungry he has filled with good things;
the rich he has sent away empty.
He has helped Israel his servant,
remembering his mercy,
according to his promise to our fathers,
to Abraham and to his descendants forever."

Luke 1:46-55

Before the Story

Before we begin, I have written this book to honor God and the Virgin Mary and to propagate a deep devotion to Mary for everybody – including myself.

In this book, I try to explain who Mary is, how important she is, what her role is, and how she can guide us to God. I first try to introduce the reader to some of the church's teachings about Mary. Then I try to tell her story before time itself and then her life in the scriptures.

Finally, I try telling her story after her death and assumption to Heaven and some of her apparitions.

There is so much to tell and so many stories that multiple books would be necessary to explain and tell as much as possible. However, since I only focused on writing one book, I will focus on some of her many apparitions.

Therefore, I will only focus on some of the stories of her actual apparitions and not any stories about other miracles done through other means.

Of course, there are so many apparitions that I will overlook some, not know about many of them, and omit others since I am trying to condense as much as possible into this one book. However, I hope that this book gives us all a chance to know and appreciate Mary deeper and create a wonderful devotion to her.

I could add so much more to this introduction but let us read the story to find out more and fill out many gaps.

Let us begin.

Mary Throughout Infinity

Part 1
The Creation of Heaven & Earth

Origins

In the beginning, God existed as one. The Father, Son, and the Holy Spirit. The Father loved the Son. The Son loved the Father and the Holy Spirit was their love manifested. Together, they form the Holy Trinity.

All three persons were complete and were one. They had no need of anything or anybody to fulfill their happiness.

However, so great was God's love that He wished to share their happiness with many creatures created in His image.

Before God created anything, He hovered in the nothingness but in Himself. Therefore, God knew that He had to create a world and home to those who would join Him in the Beatific Vision.

He began His creation by forming the Heavens and the Earth. God wanted to have many hierarchies of children: spiritual and corporeal.

Since God is spiritual, He created the spiritual beings first. These beings would be known as Angels.

In an instant, an infinite amount of Angels were created. Each Angel belonged to a certain hierarchy of the Angelic Choirs.

The closest angels to God were the Seraphim (meaning burning ones) who burned with true love for God. They incessantly blessed and proclaimed God's glory by chanting, "'Holy, holy, holy is the LORD Almighty; the whole earth is full of his glory.'" (Isaiah 6:3).

After them, the second choir became known as the Cherubim. These angels possessed infinite knowledge of God.

The third choir became known as the Thrones. Their function was to become the throne of God where He dwells in.

The fourth group was the Dominations who would become translators of God's will to the lower levels of angels.

The fifth group would become known as the Powers. Their mission would be to protect God's people and the church.

The sixth group was the Virtues who would be in charge of the elements of nature.

The seventh group was to be known as the Principalities for they were to govern different places of creation.

The eighth group was known as the Archangels. They were the ones in charge of delivering God's special messages.

The last choir was simply the angels. These beings would be in charge of looking out for individuals as their special guardians.

God created them on the first day and the Angels became the children of light.

Each of these beings was created pure and holy without sin. However, God wanted to immerse them into the Beatific Vision.

Therefore, God put them to the test to see who wanted to follow Him truly and wholeheartedly and who would reject Him.

The test that God was going to put them through was the Incarnation of Jesus through a human being.

Humans are the lowest in the spiritual realm so God wanted to see if the Angels would worship Him as a human and accept His mother as their queen.

"A great sign appeared in heaven: a woman clothed with the sun, with the moon under her feet and a crown of twelve stars on her head. She was pregnant and cried out in pain as she was about to give birth." (Revelations 12: 1-2)

For the first time ever, there was great silence in Heaven as the Angels contemplated God's revelation.

The highest Angel was Lucifer. He possessed such graces and

beauty that no other Angel could be compared to him.

Therefore, he was the key figure in this test. Would the Angels follow God or would they follow themselves and Lucifer?

What would seem like an eternity for humanity was only an instant for the Angels and they immediately chose sides?

Lucifer shouted "No!" and led a third of the Angels from every choir into a revolt against God.

He wanted to destroy God's holy chosen mother and Jesus so he set out to do so.

> "Then another sign appeared in heaven: an enormous red dragon with seven heads and ten horns and seven crowns on its heads.
> Its tail swept a third of the stars out of the sky and flung them to the earth. The dragon stood in front of the woman who was about to give birth, so that it might devour her child the moment he was born."

(Revelations 12: 3-4)

However, there was a lowly Angel from the eighth choir. His name would be known as Michael.

With a soft but firm "Yes" he shouted a cry of complete obedience and love for God.

His acceptance was a shout saying, "Who is like unto God?"

Many Angels followed St. Michael in his obedience.

> "Then war broke out in heaven. Michael and his angels fought against the dragon, and the dragon and his angels fought back. But he was not strong enough, and they lost their place in heaven. The great dragon was hurled down—that ancient serpent called the devil, or Satan, who leads the whole world astray. He was hurled to the earth, and his angels with him.

(Revelations 12: 7-9)

The woman was Mary had been born without sin and without blemish so God the Father chose her to become the mother of His only Son, Jesus.

Mary gave birth to Jesus and God bestowed every grace possible upon her. She received so much grace that no Angel could comprehend the immense power that God had bestowed on Mary.

God separated the good Angels (children of light) from the devil's followers (children of darkness).

God saw that the light (Angels) were good and together with them, He set out to finish His creation and create mankind.

[1]

---

[1] Bible Study Tools. Salem Web Network. (https://www.biblestudytools.com/revelation/12.html). September 9, 2018.

Prophesy of the Mother of God

God continued with His creation and finally made man on the sixth day.

He named the man Adam and gave him dominion over all creation on Earth.

God saw that Adam was lonely so He created many different kinds of animals.

This pleased Adam and softened his pain but he still felt lonely.

Finally, God made Adam fall into a deep sleep and removed one of his ribs.

From that rib, He created another human being to be with Adam. She became known as Eve and became Adam's wife.

God had tested the Angels so that they themselves could choose to remain with Him or not.

Therefore, He also put Adam and Eve one rule to prove their love and obedience towards Him.

God had placed a tree, known as the tree of knowledge, and forbade Adam and Eve to eat of its fruit.

The devil was envious of mankind and the love that they received from God so he was determined to corrupt mankind and turn them away from God.

The devil went about doing this by taking the form of a snake and hiding in the tree.

When Eve was alone, he seduced her and tricked her into eating the fruit. Then she passed the fruit on to Adam, which caused him to sin as well.

As soon as they ate, they lost God's grace and realized that they were now naked. When God found out that Adam and Eve had sinned, He punished them by exiling them from the Garden of Eden.

Then God looked at the devil to condemn him for his treachery saying,

"… 'Because thou hast done this, thou *art* cursed above all cattle, and above every beast of the field; upon thy belly shalt thou go, and dust shalt thou eat all the days of thy life:

And I will put enmity between thee and the woman, and between thy seed and her seed; it shall bruise thy head, and thou shalt bruise his heel.'"

(Genesis 3: 14-15)

Therefore, God told the devil that the woman, Mary, from their vision/trial, would greater than he would ever be.

And thus, here is where Mary's full mission was foretold. [2]

---

[2] King James Bible. (https://www.kingjamesbibleonline.org/Genesis-Chapter-3/). September 10, 2018.

Mary Throughout Infinity

Part 2
The Life of the Blessed Virgin Mary

Mary's Beginning

Mary's story begins with her parents were Joachim and Anne. Joachim and Anne were childless and already advanced in age. Even though they were both very pious and generous people, they had not been able to conceive a child.

This made them outcasts since people saw them as cursed and "not loved by God." However, they remained steady and kept their faith and devotion to God. God had a very special mission for them and so He wanted to test their faith.

When God saw that it was fit, He sent an angel to Joachim and Anne separately to announce the birth of Mary. Joachim and Anne were very grateful to God for a child that they offered Mary up to the Lord, thus beginning Mary's service to God.

---

[3] Camille, Alice L. "Mary's parents aren't mentioned in the Bible. How do we know their names?" Questions Catholics Ask. Vision: Vocation Network. June 30, 2015. (https://www.vocationnetwork.org/en/blog/questions_catholics_ask/2015/06/marys_parents_arent_mentioned_in_the_bible_how_do_we_know_their_names). September 28, 2018.

The Prophesy is Fulfilled

Six months had passed since the Archangel St. Gabriel appeared to Zacharias. He was still mute but his wife was in her sixth month of pregnancy.

Now it was time to finally bring forth the Messiah, but first God needed to ask a young virgin if she would take the mission to be His mother.

When God the Father decided that it was time for Jesus to come into the world, He sent the Archangel, St. Gabriel, to deliver the gift of giving birth to God's only Son.

Early one morning, Mary was deep in prayer when all of a sudden, there was a blinding bright light that illuminated her whole room. Mary covered her eyes at first and then slowly opened them to see what had caused such graceful light. When Mary's eyes adjusted to the light, she saw a man who was dressed in linen and wore a girded of gold on his waist.

His body was like beryl and his face and appearance were as bright as strong lightning. His eyes were like torches of fire. His arms and feet were burnished with a bronze color.

Mary was afraid of such a vision but the man softly spoke to her saying, "'Greetings, you who are highly favored! The Lord is with you.'" (Luke 1:28)

His voice was deep and sounded like sweet thunder.

Mary was puzzled at the kind of greeting she received from the man but remained quiet to see what the man would say next.

The man identified himself as St. Gabriel the Archangel and said:

She was confused by the type of greeting from the archangel but did not respond to it.

St. Gabriel continued his message, "(…) 'Do not be afraid, Mary, for you have found favor with God. And behold, you will conceive in your womb and bring forth a Son, and shall call His name JESUS. He will be great, and will be called the Son of the Highest; and the Lord God will give Him the throne of His father David. And He will reign over the house of Jacob forever, and of His kingdom there will be no end.'"

(Luke 1: 30-33)

Mary was more confused now and asked the archangel how that would be possible because she wasn't married yet and was still a virgin.

St. Gabriel answered her saying,

"(…) '*The* Holy Spirit will come upon you, and the power of the Highest will overshadow you; therefore, also, that Holy One who is to be born will be called the Son of God. Now indeed, Elizabeth your relative has also conceived a son in her old age; and this is now the sixth month for her who was called barren. For with God nothing will be impossible.'"

(Luke 1:35-37)

For the second time since the trial of the angels, all Heaven and earth (angels and demons) were silent again. Nothing could be heard for an instant that seemed like an eternity. Would she accept God's will or reject it?

Mary didn't fully understand but she had total faith in God so she fully immersed herself according to God's wishes towards her saying,

"… 'I am the Lord's servant. Let this thing you have said happen to me!" (Luke 1:38)

Finally, she answered, "(…) 'Behold the maidservant of the

Lord! Let it be to me according to your word.' (...)" (Luke 1:38)

When she accepted God's will and the gift of carrying His only son, St. Gabriel departed and prepared himself for the next mission that God would be sending him on next.

The fall of mankind happened through an evil Angel, a man, and a woman. Now salvation had begun through an Angel, Jesus, and Mary.

---

[4] Bible Gateway. (https://www.biblegateway.com/passage/?search=Luke+1&version=ERV). September 10, 2018.

Mychal, Rayfiel G. *Angels Throughout the Bible: The Story of the Unsung Heroes.*

Blessed Among Women

The Archangel Gabriel had informed Mary that her cousin, Elizabeth, was pregnant so Mary set forth to Judea.

Elizabeth was already advanced in years and was considered to be barren but by God's mercy and grace, she was going to give birth to St. John the Baptist.

Mary had barely arrived at the property of Zechariah when she saw Elizabeth doing her daily chores outside of her home.

Mary was excited and immediately called out to Elizabeth.

Elizabeth heard Mary's voice clearly and immediately, her unborn son started to leap inside her stomach.

Immediately, Elizabeth and her baby received the Holy Spirit and rejoiced.

Elizabeth ran towards Mary and told her,

"… 'Blessed *art* thou among women, and blessed *is* the fruit of thy womb.

And whence *is* this to me, that the mother of my Lord should come to me?

For, lo, as soon as the voice of thy salutation sounded in mine ears, the babe leaped in my womb for joy.

And blessed *is* she that believed: for there shall be a performance of those things which were told her from the Lord.'"

(Luke 1: 42-45)

Mary's heart was filled with joy and love for God. She raised her eyes up to Heaven and said:

"… 'My soul doth magnify the Lord,

And my spirit hath rejoiced in God my Saviour.

For he hath regarded the low estate of his handmaiden: for, behold, from henceforth all generations shall call me blessed.

For he that is mighty hath done to me great things; and holy *is* his name.

And his mercy *is* on them that fear him from generation to generation.

He hath shewed strength with his arm; he hath scattered the proud in the imagination of their hearts.

He hath put down the mighty from *their* seats, and exalted them of low degree.

He hath filled the hungry with good things; and the rich he hath sent empty away.

He hath holpen his servant Israel, in remembrance of *his* mercy;

As he spake to our fathers, to Abraham, and to his seed for ever."'

(Luke 1: 46-55)

    Mary continued her mission with Elizabeth and remained with her until St. John the Baptist was born and then returned home.

---

[5] King James Bible Online. (https://www.kingjamesbibleonline.org/Luke-Chapter-1/). September 10, 2018.

In a Dream

When Mary returned to her home to her parents and to her spouse, Joseph.

Mary and Joseph weren't fully married yet and so they hadn't had any physical contact. However, when Mary returned, Joseph and her parents saw that she was pregnant.

Joseph thought that Mary had been unfaithful to him so he thought that their marriage wasn't going to work out. Joseph was an honest and God fearing man so he wanted to divorce Mary quietly to avoid giving her shame and a public stoning.

However, the Archangel Gabriel appeared to Joseph in a dream to ease by telling him:

"… 'Joseph, thou son of David, fear not to take unto thee Mary thy wife: for that which is conceived in her is of the Holy Ghost.

And she shall bring forth a son, and thou shalt call his name JESUS: for he shall save his people from their sins.

Now all this was done, that it might be fulfilled which was spoken of the Lord by the prophet, saying,

Behold, a virgin shall be with child, and shall bring forth a son, and they shall call his name Emmanuel, which being interpreted is, God with us.

(Matthew 1: 20-23)

Joseph understood that God had chosen Mary for a very special mission. He also understood that God had also chosen him to be the protector and guardian of both Mary and Jesus. Therefore, Joseph woke up from his sleep and did as St. Gabriel had commanded him to do. [6]

---

[6] King James Bible Online. (https://www.kingjamesbibleonline.org/Matthew-Chapter-1/). September 10, 2018.

No Room at the Inn

During the time of Mary's pregnancy, Caesar Augustus called forth a census so Joseph had to go to Bethlehem to register there since he was of David's lineage. So Joseph packed up everything and took Mary with him to Bethlehem.

As they were approaching Bethlehem, Mary began to cry in pains of labor. Jesus was about to be born so Joseph had to find a place for Mary to deliver her baby. Joseph knocked at several inns but since many people were also traveling for the census so there weren't any places available for Mary to give birth or even spend the night. However, the owner of a manger heard of Mary's need so he offered her the manger so that she could have the room and privacy.

As soon as Mary had given birth to Jesus, St. Gabriel went to the shepherds who were out on the field. St. Gabriel appeared along with many Angels who were singing praises because Jesus had been born.

Together they sang, "'Glory to God in the highest, and on earth peace, good will toward men.'" (Luke 2: 14)

The shepherds were scared when they saw St. Gabriel and almost fled.

However. St Gabriel calmed them and brought them the good news about Jesus by saying:

"… 'Fear not: for, behold, I bring you good tidings of great joy, which shall be to all people.

For unto you is born this day in the city of David a Saviour, which is Christ the Lord.

And this *shall be* a sign unto you; Ye shall find the babe wrapped in swaddling clothes, lying in a manger.'"

(Luke 2: 10-12)

As soon as St. Gabriel and the Angels disappeared, the shepherds ran towards the manger to see the good news that they had received from God.

When they arrived at the manger, they found Joseph and Mary, cradling Jesus. They spoke about the Angels and their message and spread the good news about God being born.

Three wise men also came from the east to pay homage to Jesus. They had been following a star that was prophesized that would lead them to a future king. When they entered the manger, they fell down at the feet of Jesus and worshipped Him. They also offered Him three gifts that were gold, and frankincense, and myrrh.

Mary carefully observed everything and contemplated the amazing miracles that were happening to her and to Jesus. [7]

---

[7] King James Bible Online. (https://www.kingjamesbibleonline.org/Luke-Chapter-2/). September 10, 2018.

The Prophecy of Sorrows

Eight days after Jesus' birth, Mary and Joseph took Him to the temple to be circumcised and presented to God at the Temple. Here, Mary and Joseph did as St. Gabriel had commanded them and so they named the child Jesus.

There was a wise old man, Simeon, at the temple that day. He was very pious who had received a message from the Holy Spirit telling him that he would not die without seeing the Lord. As soon as Mary and Joseph arrived at the temple, Simeon was led by the Holy Spirit to where Jesus was.

Simeon saw Jesus and praised God saying,

"'Lord, now lettest thou thy servant depart in peace, according to thy word: For mine eyes have seen thy salvation, Which thou hast prepared before the face of all people; A light to lighten the Gentiles, and the glory of thy people Israel.'"

(Luke 2; 29-32)

Mary and Joseph were astonished at what Simeon was saying and thanking God. Simeon turned to Mary and Joseph and foretold Jesus' mission by telling them, "'Behold, this *child* is set for the fall and rising again of many in Israel; and for a sign which shall be spoken against;'" (Luke 2:34)

Then he turned to Mary and foretold to her that she would also share in Jesus' sacrifice and death by telling her, "… 'a sword shall pierce through thy own soul also,) that the thoughts of many hearts may be revealed.'" (Luke 2:35) This was the first sorrow that Mary felt as she was told that Jesus was born to her into this world to suffer and that she too would join Jesus in His pains and sacrifice on the cross. [8]

---

[8] King James Bible Online. (https://www.kingjamesbibleonline.org/Luke-Chapter-2/). September 11, 2018.

The Slaughter of the Innocents

After the purification of Mary and the presentation of Jesus at the temple, Joseph received a message from the Archangel St. Gabriel.

St. Gabriel warned Joseph telling him, "… 'Arise, and take the young child and his mother, and flee into Egypt, and be thou there until I bring thee word: for Herod will seek the young child to destroy him.'"

(Matthew 2:13)

Joseph did as St. Gabriel had instructed him to and immediately escaped with Mary and Jesus.

Herod was furious when he found out that the three wise men did not return to him to tell him about where Jesus was. In his anger, he ordered that every boy younger than two years old to be slaughtered. Thus, the night was filled with lamentations and weeping as the children were being slaughtered. [9]

---

[9] King James Bible Online. (https://www.kingjamesbibleonline.org/Matthew-Chapter-2/). September 11, 2018.

At My Father's House

Jesus grew in age willed with wisdom and the grace of God.

Each year, the Jewish people had the custom to visit the Temple every year on the feast of Passover. When Jesus was twelve years old, His parents went to Jerusalem for the feast of the Passover. Jesus, Mary, and Joseph completed the required days and celebration of the Passover and returned home. However, Jesus remained behind in Jerusalem.

Meanwhile, His parents traveled in a caravan back home and thought that Jesus was trailing around with some of His friends. However, as the day went on, His parents started looking for Him. When they realized that Jesus was not traveling with the caravan, they turned back and returned to Jerusalem. Mary and Joseph looked all over Jerusalem for three whole days. The desperation and the thought of not seeing Jesus again, Mary was struck with her second sorrow.

On the third day of their search, they finally found Jesus. They found Him in the Temple, sitting in the midst of the church priests and leaders. Jesus was interacting with the leaders of the Temple. He heard them, asked them questions, and sharing His knowledge with them.

As soon as Mary saw Jesus, she ran towards Jesus and hugged Him.

She was sobbing and asked Jesus, "…'Son, why hast thou thus dealt with us? behold, thy father and I have sought thee sorrowing.'" (Luke 2:48)

Jesus looked at her and responded, "… 'How is it that ye sought me? wist ye not that I must be about my Father's business?'" (Luke 2:49).

Mary and Joseph did not understand what Jesus meant by

those words. However, Mary kept Jesus' words in her heart and pondered on them.

    Mary and Joseph took Jesus and went back to Nazareth. Jesus continued living with His parents until it was time for Him to begin His ministry. [10]

---

[10] King James Bible Online. (https://www.kingjamesbibleonline.org/Luke-Chapter-2/). September 11, 2018.

Mary the Intercessor

Mary's first intercession for mankind to Jesus was when they attended a wedding at Cana of Galilee.

While the wedding was taking place, Mary heard that the hosts had run out of wine and were panicking since the wedding feast had to continue. Mary immediately ran to Jesus to ask Him to help the host by creating more wine for them.

Jesus responded by telling her that His mission had not yet begun but He knew that He could not refuse Mary anything for He himself along with the Father, and the Holy Spirit had given her great authority and power. Therefore, out of love for His mother, Jesus agreed to do as she wished.

Mary turned to the servants and told them to do as Jesus commanded them.

Jesus told them to fill up six jugs with water and to bring them to Him. Jesus blessed the jugs and instructed the servants to take them to the governor.

The governor was astonished that the wine that was brought to him was sweeter than the previous one. Usually, the hosts gave out the good wine first and then they would serve the other wine.

Here is when Mary first interceded for mankind and would continue to do so for all eternity. [11]

---

[11] King James Bible Online. (https://www.kingjamesbibleonline.org/John-Chapter-2/). September 16, 2018.

The Sentence is Death

Mary became the Mother of God and just like Jesus, she also had to suffer for the salvation of mankind. Mary's passion began when she heard the news that Jesus had been arrested and taken to Caiaphas and to the high priests for questioning.

Many Jews gathered outside of the Temple as Jesus had been dragged in by the Temple's guards.

Mary, along with Mary Magdalene and St. John the apostle, also joined the crowd and eagerly waited to hear the news about Jesus. Every moment that passed seemed like an eternity and with each passing second, her heart felt such immense pain that was indescribable.

There was a commotion going on inside of the Temple and soon she saw the soldiers dragging Jesus out of the Temple and headed towards Pontius Pilate's castle. The crowd was huge and Mary had no way of contacting Jesus, but nevertheless, she began to follow Jesus.

The Jewish priests entered the castle of Pontius Pilate to condemn Jesus to die.

Mary and the other bystanders stayed outside of the gates again waiting to hear the news about Jesus.

Again, it seemed like an eternity passed by as Jesus was being questioned by Pontius Pilate. Finally, Pontius Pilate came out from his office to address the crowd. He told them that he didn't find any fault in Jesus so he was going to set them free.

"Crucify Him!" yelled the crowd.

Pontius Pilate didn't want to harm Jesus so he brought out a prisoner by the name of Barabbas and asked them who they wanted him to release.

Mary, Mary Magdalene, and St. John shouted Jesus' name but the crowd drowned their votes and replied "Barabbas!"

Pontius Pilate tried again and asked the crowd who they wanted to be released.

Again, the crowd shouted for Pontius Pilate to release Barabbas.

Pontius Pilate tried bargaining with the crowd again but they insisted that he should have Jesus killed. Pontius Pilate didn't want to kill Jesus so he told his lieutenants to scourge Jesus so that the crowd could see Jesus suffering in pain satiate their thirst for blood. The soldiers did as Pontius Pilate ordered and took Jesus away.

Mary tried to find a way to get close to Jesus and witness where they were going to take Him.

However, the crowd was large and Jesus was taken to the courtyard of the castle where the Romans punished their enemies.

Mary was anxious and wanted so desperately to see Jesus. However, as soon as the soldiers brought Him out, she almost fainted at the sight of Him. He was beaten beyond recognition. His whole body was covered in blood and his face was also covered with bruises along with blood that oozed from the crown of thorns.

Mary would've fainted and died of pain as she saw how Jesus was tortured, but the grace of God strengthened her.

Pontius Pilate hoped that the crowd would be appeased not that Jesus was on the verge of death. However, the crowd continued to yell "Crucify Him!"

Pontius Pilate pleaded with them to have mercy on Jesus, but the more he did so, the more violent the crowd was. Finally, Pontius Pilate realized that he had no other choice. The mob was going to turn violent so he gave his lieutenants orders to carry out the mob's wishes and crucify Jesus.

Mary realized that there was no going back now. She

would never hold her son, Jesus, in her arms again to bring Him comfort.

[12]

---

[12] King James Bible Online. (https://www.kingjamesbibleonline.org/John-Chapter-19/). September 16, 2018.

The Way of the Cross

Pontius Pilate ordered his soldiers to carry out the wishes of the high priests and crucify Jesus. The soldiers brought Jesus a heavy cross made out of wood, which He was to carry to cavalry to be crucified in.

Mary saw how weak Jesus was and how He could barely stand after He had been scourged. Nonetheless, Jesus was forced to carry the cross.

Mary would've done everything she could to save Jesus, even if it meant that she carry the cross herself. However, she knew that this was God's will so she patiently and sorrowfully accepted.

Jesus was suffering physically and mentally as He carried the cross, and Mary suffered alongside with Him to become a co-redeemer with Jesus.

The crowd gathered and followed Jesus as He exited the city with the cross over His shoulder. Many people in the crowd threw stones, spits, and curses at Jesus. At the same time, Mary herself felt every ounce of pain alongside Jesus. Jesus was at His lowest both physically and mentally and in His weakness, He fell as He was carrying the cross.

As soon as Jesus fell, Mary ran to Him to console Him. There was so much that she wanted to do to console Him and help Him. Her only son was suffering and in desperate need of consolation. This made her heart break even more and even she herself would fallen alongside with Jesus. However, Jesus gave her a look of compassion and gratitude. Jesus was suffering while in His passion but when He saw how much His mother was suffering with Him, He wanted to hold her so that they could console each other.

The encountered that Jesus shared with Mary gave Him the strength to stand up and pick up His cross again.

Jesus could barely stand and many feared that He would die on the way, so the soldiers forced a man by the name of Simon to help Jesus carry His cross.

At the same time, Mary Magdalene and St. John helped Mary to her feet and supported her the same way that Simon helped Jesus.

Mary remembered every moment that she spent with Jesus and everything that they had shared together.

She also remembered the prophecy from Simeon who prophesized Mary's suffering. This was her fourth sorrow.

The Crucifixion

Finally, Jesus had arrived at the mountain of Golgotha, where He was going to be crucified. Mary had to suffer the humiliation of Jesus being stripped of His clothes as He was about to be crucified.

Every scream that Jesus shouted as the nails were being driven into His arms and feet caused her immense pain that she felt as though she herself was being nailed. However, the fact that her son was the one being tortured and not her caused her even more indescribable pain.

Finally when Jesus was nailed on the cross, Mary, Mary Magdalene, and St. John stood right underneath Jesus' cross.

Mary couldn't do anything for Jesus but support Him with her presence, but at the same time, she knew that her sorrows caused Jesus even more pain. Nevertheless, Jesus and Mary shared a look of love and compassion – not just for each other but also for all humanity who were greatly depending on their sacrifices for their salvation.

When Jesus was about to die, He gave Mary to be the mother of St. John and all humanity. At the same time, He gave St. John and all humanity the grace of having Mary as their mother. Jesus felt completely alone and abandoned. In His loneliness, he yelled out to the Father asked Him why He had abandoned Him. Mary felt great pain and pity as she saw how alone Jesus felt. Not only was He left alone by His disciples and followers, but now He felt completely abandoned from His own Father.

Finally, around three in the afternoon, Jesus spoke His last words and surrendered His spirit to the Father. Jesus looked at Mary with one final look of compassion and then to God the Father and perished.

Mary had finally lost Jesus and her heart was filled with such loneliness that nothing on Earth and no amount of love could ever fill it up. Nonetheless, Mary Magdalene and St. John remained with Mary to sustain her and for comfort.

Losing Jesus to death was the fifth sorrow of Mary. And so, Mary received into her Immaculate Heart all of Jesus' sufferings, His passion on the cross, His last words, and every last drop of His precious blood.

Mary offered all of her pain and Jesus' pain to God the Father so that Jesus would be glorified and for the salvation of all souls. [13]

---

[13] Pronechen, Joseph. *Our Lady's Seven Sorrows, Seven Promises, and Fatima's Connection.* National Catholic Register. SEP. 15, 2017. (HTTP://WWW.NCREGISTER.COM/BLOG/JOSEPH-PRONECHEN/OUR-LADYS-SEVEN-SORROWS-SEVEN-PROMISES-AND-FATIMAS-CONNECTION). September 17, 2018.

In the Arms of Mary

After Jesus passed away, the Roman soldiers broke the legs of the other two prisoners who were also crucified next to Jesus. The soldiers saw that Jesus was dead but they wanted to make sure so one got a spear and drove it into Jesus' side causing His last drops of blood and water to pour out.

Mary was still standing underneath the cross and saw how Jesus had given His entire self for the salvation of souls.

Once the other two thieves were dead, the soldiers brought down their bodies, as well as Jesus'. Mary immediately ran towards Jesus' body and embraced it. She embraced His body like the first time that she held Him in her arms when He was born.

She embraced Him in a protective way. And at the same time, she embraced His body knowing that it would be the last time she would be able to before letting Him go.

This was her sixth sorrow.

Jesus had completed His mission on earth, but for Mary, she would continue to suffer the events of Jesus' passion.

Farewell

There was a very devout follower of Jesus, who was a Jewish priest, by the name of Joseph of Arimathea. Joseph went to Pontius Pilate to ask if he could take possession of Jesus' body.

Pontius Pilate agreed and gave Joseph permission to take the body of Jesus. When Joseph arrived at Golgotha, where Jesus had been crucified.

When he arrived, he paid his respects to both Jesus and Mary.

At first, Mary was apprehensive when she saw Joseph because he didn't know him and confused him for one of the church elders who condemned Jesus. However, Mary felt in her heart that Joseph was trustworthy and meant no harm towards either of them.

Joseph offered Jesus a tomb that hadn't been used before. Mary agreed and Joseph had his servants carry Jesus' body to the tomb.

Once they had arrived at the tomb, they covered Jesus' body with a clean fresh linen. Then they laid Jesus' body down on a bed of stone. Mary kept her gaze on Jesus throughout the whole process. She never blinked nor strayed her eyes anywhere else. She remained standing next to Jesus as everybody else was leaving the tomb. She had no desire to leave. He was her world and she lived for Him. But now, He was gone.

This was her seventh sorrow.

Her world had come to an end and she wanted to die also so that she could be with her son again. However, she knew that her mission on earth was not over.

She had been the mother of God but now Jesus had given her to all humanity so that she could be the mother of all humanity.

Pentecost

Once Jesus had resurrected and ascended into Heaven, the apostles were hiding out fear of persecution.

On one occasion, Mary and the eleven remaining apostles were in an upper room in prayer. Mary had the Holy Spirit and shared that grace with the apostles. However, Jesus had promised to send the Holy Spirit to them so that they could finally begin their mission with all the graces and gifts possible to them.

On that occasion, there was a sudden sound coming from Heaven like mighty thunder. A wind began to rush inside the upper room where Mary and the apostles were.

Then the Holy Spirit poured out Himself in the form of tongues of fire that sat on their heads. They were immediately filled with the Holy Spirit and began to speak in many different languages. The apostles were now filled with the fire of the Holy Spirit. Now they were finally ready to go out into the world and began to spread the Gospel of the Lord.

Like a good mother, Mary let the apostles go out as a mother would let their children leave the house to begin a new life for themselves.

Even though Jesus had ascended into Heaven and the apostles were now filled with the Holy Spirit, Mary still suffered Jesus' passion. The wounds from her seven sorrows and the pain that she and Jesus felt during His passion would stay with her and torment her forever.

The Queen of Heaven

Nobody really knows what Mary's life was like after the crucifixion. However, there are many saints and scholars who have had revelations about her assumption.

Denis Vincent Wiseman recounts the events leading to her death by telling us that she was joined by the twelve apostles.

Mary received a message from an angel foretelling her her death. She tells the apostles about the message from the angels so they all gather in Jerusalem to spend Mary's final days with her.

Mary commits her soul into the hands of Jesus as she died.

The apostles buried her near Gethsemane where she is buried. The apostles also kept watching over her body for three days until they noticed that she had been taken to Heaven in body and soul.

The apostles found her tomb empty and with a scent of fresh spring flowers.

Denis Vincent Wiseman teaches us that Jesus told St. Michael to escort Mary into Heaven by saying:

"(…) 'Let them bring the body of Mary into the clouds.' And when the body of Mary had been brought into the clouds, Our Lord said to the Apostles that they should draw near to the clouds. And when they drew near to the clouds they were singing with the voices of angels. And Our Lord told the clouds to go to the gate of paradise. And when they had entered paradise, the body of Mary went to the tree of life; and they brought her soul and made it enter her body.'" (Wiseman, no pag.)

As Mary was ascending up to Heaven, a choir of innumerable angels appeared to accompany her and escort her up to Heaven.

Jesus waited for her in Heaven and when she arrived He stretched out His and received her holy and spotless body and soul.

All the angels and saints in Heaven rejoiced and together praised her by chanting, "'Blessed are you among women,'" and also sang a magnificent harmony to welcome her as their Queen. (Wiseman, no pag.)

As she ascended into Heaven, the sky shone with splendid colors and the angels in Heaven were mesmerized by her eyes and body shone with the brightest and most beautiful light.

Once she reached God's throne, Jesus the Father, and the Holy Spirit crowned her with a crown of twelve stars and officially awarded her as Queen of Heaven and the entire universe.

Now Mary's mission on earth had been fulfilled and finally became the queen of Heaven and earth.

However, as Jesus' mother, she also became the mother of all humanity and continues to take care of all humanity as their mother. [14]

---

[14] Wiseman, Denis Vincent. *Assumption Dogma the Assumption*. All About Mary. July 19, 2002. (https://www.udayton.edu/imri/mary/a/assumption-dogma.php). September 21, 2018.

First Church

After the Resurrection and the coming of the Holy Spirit, the apostles went throughout the world to share the Gospel.

St. James, who one of the twelve apostles and the brother of John, went to Galicia where he established a Christian community. St. James and his disciples were resting on the shore side of the Egro River when they started to hear sweet voices singing.

They looked around and saw that the sky was light up by a multitude of Angels. The angels were carrying the Virgin Mary on a throne. The strange fact was that at that time, the Virgin Mary was still alive and was living in Jerusalem.

This meant that she was experiencing a phenomenon known as bilocation.

Mary instructed St. James to construct a church there where God would be glorified and honored. To bless the location and the temple, she gave St. James a pillar with her image to place inside the church.

The Blessed Mother told St. James that the church would remain on earth until the end of the world. She also promised that she would bless all those who visited the church and would bless their prayers. [15]

---

[15] SCTJM. "The Relation of St. James, the Apostle, with the Blessed Virgin Mary." Treasures of the Church- Marian Shrines and Apparitions. 2006.
(http://www.piercedhearts.org/treasures/shrines/santiago.htm). September 20, 2018.

The Story of the Mother of God

Part 3
Marian Apparitions

The Virgin Mary's First Apparition

At the crucifixion, Jesus had given St. John Mary as his mother. Likewise, He also gave St. John as a son to Mary. After the crucifixion, Mary moved in with St. John and became a mother to him. However, after Mary died, St. John missed her terribly and the pain of her absence caused him much pain. The Virgin Mary saw St. John's pain and had mercy on him by appearing to him. Not only did the Virgin Mary appear to St. John, but Jesus also appeared to him. St. John was unified with the Virgin Mary in suffering since both of them stood underneath the cross.

The Virgen Mary wanted to unite the sorrows that she suffered with the rest of humanity so she asked Jesus to grant special graces to people who are devoted to her sorrows. Jesus agreed and out of love and obedience, He granted Mary's wish. Therefore, Jesus granted those who honor Mary's sorrows by promising four graces to those who are devoted.

The promises are: First, that those who before death invoke the Divine Mother in the name of her sorrows should obtain true repentance of all their sins. Second, that He would protect all who have this devotion in their tribulations, and that He would protect them especially at the hour of death. Third, that He would impress upon their minds the remembrance of His Passion, and that they should have their reward for it in heaven. Fourth, that He would commit such devout clients to the hands of Mary, with the power to dispose of them in whatever manner she might please, and to obtain for them all the graces she might desire." [16]

---

[16] Pronechen Joseph. "Our Lady's Seven Sorrows, Seven Promises, and Fatima's Connection." National Catholic Register. September 15, 2017. (http://www.ncregister.com/blog/joseph-pronechen/our-ladys-seven-sorrows-seven-promises-and-fatimas-connection). September 20, 2018.

Our Lady of Garabandal

In the evening of June 1961, four little girls experienced an apparition that would forever change their lives and the lives of millions of people

On a small town in Spain named San Sebastian of Garabandal, four little girls, (Conchita Gonzalez, Maria Dolores Mazon, Jacinta Gonzalez and Maria Cruz Gonzalez) were playing on the outskirts of their town.

Suddenly, there was the sound of great thunder followed by a spirit made of pure light. As their eyes adjusted, the spirit introduced himself as St. Michael the Archangel.

St. Michael appeared to them for several days to prepare them to see Our Lady.

Finally, a few weeks later, the Virgin Mary appeared to the children as they were playing in the field.

The Virgin Mary appeared to them on Sunday, July 2. That evening was full of bystanders who were curious to see the apparitions.

At six in the evening, the girls were standing on the hills where they had been visited by St. Michael.

The apparition began as soon as the girls went into a state of ecstasy.

The girls then saw Our Lady along with two Angels, one of them was St. Michael.

The girls explained their experience of Our Lady saying:

""""She is dressed in a white robe with a blue mantle and a crown of golden stars. Her hands are slender. There is a brown scapular on her right arm, except when she carried the Child Jesus in her arms. Her hair, deep nut-brown, is parted in the center. Her face is long, with a fine nose. Her mouth is very pretty with lips a bit thin. She looks like a girl of eighteen. She is rather tall. There is no voice like hers. No woman is just like her, either in the voice or the face or anything else. " Our Lady Manifested herself as Our Lady of Carmel.""

(St. Michael's Garabandal Center)

The girls continued to see the Virgin Mary many times a week at different times of the day.

At first, when the girls went into ecstasy, the remained kneeling but eventually they would walk or run while in that state. Even though they were moving at fast speeds through unknown places, they remained in ecstasy and ignored the world around them without getting hurt.

The girls would often receive Holy Communion from an Angel. The Angel would appear to them with a golden chalice and give them Communion on the mouth.

People witnessed these events and could see the girls gesturing and moving as if they were really receiving Holy Communion.

Once, St. Michael told them that the people would see the Host appear in the girls' mouth. Many people witnessed this event and saw actually recorded the whole event.

Conchita, one of the girls, once stated that Our Lady promised a great miracle so that everybody would come to believe and repent. However, if people didn't change their ways after the miracle, God was going to punish people directly.

On June of 1965, the day that Conchita had told people about a great sign, many people appeared at the same location where they waited to see the Virgin Mary.

Around 11:30 p.m. the girls went into ecstasy and St. Michael appeared to deliver Our Lady's message to the girls.

St. Michael reported:

""""Since my message of October 18 has not been made known to the world and has not been fulfilled, I tell you that this is my last message. Previously, the cup was being filled. Now it is overflowing. Many Cardinals, many Bishops and many Priests are on the road to perdition and with them they are bringing many souls. The Holy Eucharist is being given less importance (honor). We must avoid God's anger with us by our efforts at amendment. If we beg pardon with sincerity of soul, He will forgive us. I, your Mother, through the intercession of St. Michael the Archangel, want to tell you to amend your lives. You are already receiving one of the last warnings. I love you very much and do not want your condemnation. Ask sincerely and we will give to you. You should make more sacrifices. Think of the Passion of Jesus.""""

(St. Michael's Garabandal Center)

On Saturday, November 13, 1965, Conchita had her last apparition of Our Lady in Garabandal. On that apparition, Our Lady appeared to the children holding Baby Jesus on her hands. She told Conchita why she didn't appear the before and sent St. Michael instead. Our Lady told her that she was too sad to deliver the message herself. She told Conchita that even though the message was a hard one to deliver and receive, it must be told to save humanity. However, she told Conchita that Jesus didn't want to punish humanity and that is why she had to deliver the message.

This was the last time that the children saw Our Blessed Mother but she promised to return to them to let them know when the Great Miracle was going to take place and when the punishment would begin.

[17]

The Garabandal Story. St. Michael's Garabandal Center. <http://www.garabandal.org/story.shtml>. June 18, 2018.

Our Lady of Family Values

In 1944, Our Lady appeared to a seven-year-old girl, Adelaide Roncalli, at Torchio.

During this time, World War II was tearing Italy apart. The people prayed to the Virgin Mary for liberation since the war did not seem like it was going to end. As an answer to their prayer, the Virgin Mary appeared to Adelaide while she was out picking flowers to offer them to an image of Our Blessed Mother.

The Virgin Mary appeared, along with Baby Jesus, and Joseph. On some occasions, the Holy Family would be accompanied by angels. She described all three of them encircled in glowing lights.

The Virgin Mary was wearing a white dress with a string of pearls a golden necklace, and a blue mantle. On her right arm, she held a Rosary made of white beads and she had two roses on her bare feet.

Adelaide was about to run away but the Virgin Mary gently identified herself. However, Jesus and Joseph did not speak to her. Instead, they looked at her with loving gazes and sweet smiles.

The Virgin Mary asked Adelaide to return for nine more days.

On another apparition, Our Lady told Adelaide that she would suffer a lot in life but in the end, she would be in Heaven with her. When Adelaide reported the apparitions, she was rejected, isolated, frightened and was physiologically tortured.

Our Lady had also told her that if people repented and prayed, then the war would end in two months.

On the ninth apparition, Our Lady performed a miracle with the sun just like she had done in Fatima. Many described the event stating that the sun came out of the clouds, whirled dizzily on itself, and projected beams of multiple colors that colored everything and everybody.

The disc looked like a Host, many saw a Rosary in the sky, and others saw Our Lady's face looming in the Sun.

On her last apparition, Our Lady told Adelaide that she would suffer much in life but she would come to take her to Heaven the moment she died.

After the apparitions ended, Adelaide suffered much ridicule from the authorities – including the church authorities. Adelaide suffered such ridicule but the words from Our Lady kept her strong. Due to schemes and trickery, Adelaide's apparitions were considered lies but eventually, the truth came out and this apparition was made official.

Our Lady also recognized this apparition when she appeared in Brazil back in 1996.

---

[18][18] "Adelaide Roncalli." *The Story.* Madonna Delleghiaie. (http://www.madonnadelleghiaie.it/inglese/adelaide.asp). September 27, 2018.

"The Apparitions at Ghiaie Di Bonate (Italy)." Foundation Mary Pages.(https://www.marypages.com/ghiaie-di-bonate-(italy)-en.html). September 27, 2018.

Carpenter, John. "Our Lady of Family Values, Ghiaie Di Bonate, Italy, 1944." *Marian Apparitions.* Divine Mysteries and Miracles. August 15, 2016. (http://www.divinemysteries.info/our-lady-of-family-values-ghiaie-di-bonate-italy-1944/). September 27, 2018.

Our Lady of Mercy

In 1536, a farmer named Antonio Botta received an apparition in Savona, Italy. Antonio described that Mary was wearing a white dress and that she was surrounded by white bright light. The Virgin Mary was standing on a large rock that overlooked a river.

The Virgin Mary told Antonio to go to his priest and to request that three Saturdays should be observed as days of fasting.

Another thing that she requested was that there should be three processions on those Saturdays in honor of God and her as the Mother of Jesus.

After the three Saturdays, Mary asked the farmer to return to that place again so that she could give him another message. Antonio did as the Virgin Mary had instructed him to do and the church officials believed him and did as Antonio had related.

After the three Saturdays, Antonio returned to the designated location where he was to meet the Virgin Mary again. On this apparition, Our Lady told Antonio to set aside another three more Saturdays of fasting and processions. The Virgin Mary told Antonio that she wished for mercy and not justice. She disappeared and left a sweet fragrance of roses behind. Antonio told the church authorities and many people began to arrive at that location and built a shrine.

On May of 1815, Pope Pius VII crowned the statue of this apparition as Our Lady of Mercy. [19]

---

[19] Carpenter, John. "Our Lady of Mercy: Savona Italy (1536)." *Marian Apparitions*. Divine Mysteries and Miracles. July 16, 2016. (http://www.divinemysteries.info/our-lady-of-mercy-savona-italy-1536/). September 26, 2018.

Our Lady of Ocotlan

Ten years after Our Lady appeared to Juan Diego, Our Lady appeared to another Indian in Mexico named Juan Diego Bernardino. The apparition happened in Ocotlan where there was political unrest and smallpox was sweeping throughout Mexico and killing many people. Juan Diego worked in a Franciscan convent when he went out to find water for his sick relatives.

As he was fetching water, Our Lady appeared to him. Juan Diego was frozen as he was captivated by her beauty and her sweet smile. That is when Our Lady told Juan Diego, "… 'My heart always desires to help those who are suffering. My heart cannot bear to see so much pain and suffering among people without healing them.'" (The Catholic Travel Guide, no pag.) Our Lady guided Juan Diego to a spring of water and told him that that water would heal his relatives as well as everybody else who drinks from it. Soon after this, many people also drank and the epidemic ended.

The Virgin Mary had also told Juan Diego about an image of her that would bring forth many cures and miracles. After Juan Diego told the Franciscans about the statue, they searched for it and eventually found a forest that was on fire.

However, they noticed that one tree wasn't burning so they realized that this tree was special. The Friars saw this as a sign and took an ax to cut the tree to better investigate it. Upon cutting the tree, they found a wooden statue of the Virgin Mary. The Friars took the statue back to their monastery and placed the statue there. Today, the statue rests in the Basilica at Ocotlan. [20]

---

[20] "The apparitions of Our Lady of Ocotlan." Ocotlan, Mexico: Statue of Our Lady of Ocotlan & Healing Well of Ocotlan. The Catholic Travel Guide. (https://thecatholictravelguide.com/destinations/mexico/ocotlan-mexico-statue-lady-ocotlan-healing-well-ocotlan/). September 24, 2018.

Admin. "Our Lady of Ocotlan – "The Lourdes of Mexico", Tlaxcala, Tlax." Madonnas of Mexico. (http://madonnasofmexico.com/2011/08/01/our-lady-of-ocotlan-the-lourdes-of-mexico-tlaxcala-tlax/). September 24, 2018.

Our Lady of Saint-Cordon

On September 6, 1008, Our Lady appeared to Bertholin in Valenciennes, France.

During the time of the apparition, a terrible famine killed approximately 8,000 people in only a few days. The people were crushed by so much suffering and death that they begged Our Lady for help. Bertholin, a holy hermit, prayed fervently to Our Lady begging her to rescue her children.

Our Lady appeared to him in a light that was brighter than the sun. She told Bertholin to go to the people and ask them to fast the following day and to pray all night so that the plague would end. The people believed him and did exactly what he had told him.

The night of prayer, everybody waited for dawn to see the miracle happened. As the sun rose, Our Lady descended from Heaven in all her majesty, along with a multitude of angels.

The Virgin Mary blessed the people and all the sick were immediately healed. She also instructed Bertholin to tell the people to make a solemn procession every year in her honor to thank her.

The people did as the Virgin had requested and since then, they have held the procession every year and a shrine in Notre-Dame-la-Grande opened. [21]

---

[21] Our Lady of the Fountain. Roman Catholic Saints. (https://www.roman-catholic-saints.com/our-lady-of-the-fountain.html). September 26, 2018.

Our Lady of the Fountain, Italy

On May 1432, Our Lady appeared in Caravaggio in Lombardy, Italy to a woman named Giannetta Varoli. Giannetta Varoli was a thirty-two-year-old woman whose husband was an alcoholic. On May twenty-six, Giannetta was out on the field collecting bundles of grass for her animals. While she was on the road, the Virgin Mary appeared to her.

In this apparition, Our Lady was dressed in a blue dress and her head was covered with a white veil. The Virgin Mary was extremely sad and trying to hold back her tears. Giannetta was scared at first but the Virgin reassured her that she was the Virgin Mary.

On the verge on tears, Our Lady told Giannetta:

"'The Most High Almighty, my Son, wanted to destroy this Earth because of the iniquity of men, because they do what is evil every day and fall into sin by sin. But for seven years, I prayed mercy to the Son for their sins. Therefore, I want you to tell each and every one who you must fast on bread and water every Friday in honor of my Son, and that, after vespers, celebrate me every Saturday for devotion. That must be dedicated to me this half a day as gratitude for the many and great favors that you received from my Son through my intercession.'" (The Miracle Hunter, no pag.)

Giannetta told the Virgin Mary that nobody would believe her. However, with a tearful voice, the Virgin assured her that she would perform great miracles to prove their apparition. Giannetta did as the Virgin had asked and in 1575, the Sanctuary of Caravaggio was constructed and dedicated to Our Lady of the Fountain.[22]

---

[22] Miracle Hunter. Caravaggio, Lombardy, Italy (1432): Madonna del Fonte (Our Lady of the Fountain). Marian Apparitions. Miracle Hunter.com (http://www.marianapparitions.org/marian_apparitions/approved_apparitions/caravaggio/index.html) September 26, 2018.

Our Lady of the Miraculous Medal

On January 1842, a man Marie Alphonse Ratisbonne, who was a Jew saw the Virgin Mary after a life of hatred towards Catholics.

Marie was born as a Jew and his family also practiced the Jewish faith. He hated the Catholics because his brother George had converted to Christianity and had become a priest.

During an argument about Christianity with a baron who challenged Marie to wear the Miraculous Medal.

Marie and the Baron had a friend, Comte de la Ferronays, who had been ill and praying for the conversion of Marie. While Comte was praying for Marie, he had a heart attack and died. The Baron asked Marie if he could help him arrange the funeral arrangements for their deceased friend.

Marie was waiting inside a church to admire the artwork. When he was about to leave, a huge black dog appeared and was ready to attack him. Marie froze in terror and just as the dog was about to attack, a bright light chased it away.

Marie turned around and saw that the light came directly from the Virgin Mary who had appeared to him. The Blessed Mother was wearing a crown and a long white tunic with a jeweled belt around her waist and a blue-green mantle that was draped over her left shoulder.

The light was so bright and enchanting that Marie had to look away. Marie felt that the bright rays from the Virgin Mary contained the secrets of Divine Pity.

Our Lady didn't say anything but Marie understood her message and fell down to his knees and began to cry.

When the Baron walked into the church, he found Marie crying. Marie immediately told the Baron that he wanted to convert to Christianity.

Eventually, he joined the priesthood and focused on converting Jews.[23]

---

[23] "Our Lady of the Miracle / Our Lady of Zion." Rome, Italy. *The Miracle Hunter.* (http://www.miraclehunter.com/marian_apparitions/approved_apparitions/rome1842/index.html). September 24, 2018.

"Our Lady of the Miraculous Medal, Rome, Italy 1842, *Marian Apparitions.* Divine Mysteries and Miracles. (http://www.divinemysteries.info/our-lady-of-the-miraculous-medal-rome-italy-1842/). September 24, 2018.

The Mother of True Lights

On March 25, 1986, the Holy Virgin Mary appeared in a church in Cairo Egypt.

In the evening, Mary appeared beside the two towers of the church of St. Demiana. She shone in bright light and an even brighter halo.

This apparition was witnessed by the people living in that area.

Because of the nature of her apparition, Mary became known as The Mother of True Lights.However, news began to spread and thousands of people began to visit the church.

The apparitions continued up until 1991.[24]

---

[24] "The Apparitions of the Blessed Holy Virgin Mary in the Church of Saint Demiana the Martyr, In Papadouplo, Shoubra, Cairo, Egypt (1986-1991)." Zeitoun Web Gallery. (http://www.zeitun-eg.org/demiana.htm). September 23, 2018.

Apparition to Elizabeth Canori Mora

On Christmas day of 1816, Our Lady appeared to Elizabeth Canori Mora to show her an apocalyptic vision.

Elizabeth saw Baby Jesus bleeding from the persecutions and sins from humanity.

She also saw wolves dressed as sheep and were ready to destroy and devour the pope and the church.

She saw how the Eternal Father's face was full of anger with His hand ready to strike the earth.

The Virgin Mary appeared to her in tears and told her that she had stopped asking Jesus for mercy and instead she was pleading to the Father for Justice. God the Father unleashed all the demons from Hell and unleashed them into the world to punish all of His enemies.

This vision happened almost a century before the Fatima apparitions, yet it reflects the same message that she gave in Fatima. Our Lady foretold that destruction and chaos that was going to take place in the 20th century. [25]

---

[25] "A Century Before Fatima, Providence Announced a Chastisement." *Catholic Perspective*. The American Society for the Defense of Tradition, Family, and Property. April 10, 2007. (http://www.tfp.org/a-century-before-fatima-providence-announced-a-chastisement/). September 27, 2018.

Evensong. "The Prophecy of Blessed Elizabeth Canori Mora." Return to Fatima: In the End, my Immaculate Heart will Triumph. September 17, 2018. (https://www.returntofatima.org/2015/09/the-prophecy-of-blessed-elizabeth-canori-mora/). September 27, 2018.

Mother of the Word

In the early 1980s, Our Lady appeared in Rwanda, Africa, to seven children;

Alphonsine Mumureke, Marie-Claire Mukangang, Stephanie Mukamurenzi, Agnes Kamagaju, Emanuel Segatashya, and Vestine Salima.

However, the Virgin Mary appeared to each child individually at different times and different places.

The first one to see the Virgin Mary was Alphonsine as she was serving lunch to her friends.

Our Lady introduced herself as the "Mother of the Word." She described the Virgin Mary as the most beautiful woman who wore a white seamless dress and a white veil on her head. The children would go into states of ecstasies when they were witnessing the apparitions. In each apparition, Our Lady would perform several different signs to certify her apparitions.

On one apparition, the Virgin Mary made the sun dance across the sky. The dancing sun created several colors like a rainbow that was swirling in a glass circle. Then there appeared another sun behind it. Then the Eucharist and chalice appeared on the moon and the colors changed again.

A third sun appeared that was red, green, and gold.

Then the face of Mary appeared in the center of the sun.

Our Lady pleaded with them to pray the Rosary and to promote it because the Rwanda Genocide was about to begin.

After the first apparitions, Our Lady appeared to them sad and sorrowful. In turn, the seven children cried, trembled, and their teeth chattered in fear.

In the apparitions, the children saw rivers of blood, people killing each other, dead people lying around abandoned, trees in flames, bodies without limbs, and decapitated heads.

The vision became reality in 1994 when the Rwanda Genocide took place and slaughtered more than 500,000 people.

Marie-Claire was killed in the town of Byumba in the summer of 1994. Emanuel died while running away from Kigali. Segatashya also died in the Holocaust.

After years of investigations after the genocide, the Pope and the Vatican added the apparitions of Rwanda to the list of approved Marian apparition sites.[26]

---

[26] Carpenter, John. "Our Lady of Kibeho, Rwanda, Africa, 1981-1989." *Marian Apparitions*. September 1, 2016. (http://www.divinemysteries.info/our-lady-of-kibeho-rwanda-africa-1981-1989/). September 28, 2018.

Clemente-Arnaldo, Nora V. "Our Lady's Apparition in Rwanda, Africa." *Totus Tuus, Maria!* (http://www.all-about-the-virgin-mary.com/marian-apparitions-rwanda.html). September 28, 2018.

Jones, Michael K. "The Apparitions of Our Lady of Kibeho, Rwanda." Medjugorje USA. (http://www.medjugorjeusa.org/rwanda.htm). September 28, 2018.

Our Lady of EDSA

During the 1980s in the Philippines, there was political tension that was threatening the inhabitants that almost led to a massacre.

Ferdinand Marcos was a corrupt dictator who received power after rigged elections. Millions of people went into the streets to protest and attempting a coup.

A small group of the military also joined in the coup but when Marcos discovered them, he ordered his army to kill them. He sent his whole army, along with tanks and other armed vehicles.

The Archbishop of Manila, Cardinal Jaime Sin, heard of the upcoming massacre and mobilized the people to go out into the streets and protect them. The people, including priests and nuns, took to the streets but did not take any weapons to fight against the army.

Instead, they all brought their Rosaries, flowers, food, and images of the Virgin Mary. They all sang and prayed the Rosary so that the Virgin Mary would protect them.

The soldiers were ready to kill the masses to protect Marcos' regime, but as soon as they were face to face with the protesters, a cross appeared in the sky. However, this did not stop the army from advancing. The people continued to pray and sing the Ave Maria.

Suddenly, a white dazzling light appeared and from within, a beautiful woman appeared in front of the tanks. The beautiful woman was the Virgin Mary who wore a blue dress.

She extended her arms forward and spoke in a loud yet gentle voice. The Virgin Mary told them to stop and not to harm her children.

The soldiers were filled with terror so they dropped their weapons and joined the masses that were against the Marcos regime. Marcos knew that he had lost all power so he immediately fled the Philippines.

After this apparition, a church was built in honor of Mary known as Our Lady of the Shrine of EDSA (Epifanio de Los Santos Avenue).

---

[27] Francis, Tej. "Marian Apparitions (75) – Manila, Philippines" Oclarim. July 20, 2018. (http://www.oclarim.com.mo/en/2018/07/20/marian-apparitions-75-manila-philippines/). September 30, 2018.

Our Lady of Gietrzwald

On June 27, 1877, Our Lady appeared to Justyna Szafrynska while she was walking home from church with her mother. Even though Our Lady appeared to Justyna Szafrynska while she was with her mother, only she could see the Holy Virgin.

The Virgin Mary asked Justyna to return the following day. Justyna did but she brought along her friend, Barbara Samulowska, who was also able to see her.

The girls described Our Lady as being very bright and sitting on a throne with the Child Jesus sitting among angels, who crowned her, over a maple tree. Our Lady introduced herself as "The Most Holy Virgin Mary Immaculately Conceived" The Virgin Mary asked the girls to pray the Rosary fervently and pray for the salvation of sinners. The Blessed Mother told the girls that if people prayed, she would send priests into the empty churches throughout Poland and protect the church from her enemies.

Justyna asked the Virgin Mary if she would heal people. Our Lady blessed a spring of water and told the girls that through it, many people would be healed, both physically and spiritually.

On her last apparition, Our Lady blessed a statue of herself that was in a small chapel. She promised the girls that she would bless everybody who asked for it. As she was leaving, she told the girls to keep praying the Holy Rosary.

The church approved this apparition on 1977 and designated a Basilica Minor in Gietrzwald by Pope Paul VI. [28]

---

[28] "The Holy Mother Appears in Gietrzwald, Poland (In 1877)." *Gietrzwald (Poland) 1877*. Foundation Mary Pages. (https://www.marypages.com/gietrzwald-(poland)-en.html). September 28, 2018.

Lamiroy, Manuel. "Our Lady of Gietrzwald, Poland, 1877. *Marian Apparitions*. Divine Mysteries and Miracles. (http://www.divinemysteries.info/our-lady-of-gietrzwald-poland-1877/). September 28, 2018.

Our Lady of Pellevoisin

In February of 1876, the Virgin Mary appeared to a young woman named Estelle Faguette, while she was on her deathbed.

During that time, Estelle was dying from tuberculosis and only had hours to live. While she was in bed, she saw a demon crawling near her bed.

However, Our Lady appeared to her and the demon immediately fled. Not only did this occur once, but also the devil would appear to her every time that the Virgin Mary would appear to her.

Our Lady cured her and told her that she would suffer in life but that would give her glory as well as Estelle. However, Our Lady kept encouraging her to stay strong and to have courage. However, at times she would gently reprimand her to help Estelle reach a state of spiritual maturity.

The Virgin Mary also told Estelle to pray because she could no longer hold God's anger so France would suffer a lot. In her appearances, the Virgin Mary wore a white robe and a scapular with the image of the Sacred Heart of Jesus.

The Virgin Mary told Estelle to propagate the devotion of the Sacred Heart. Our Blessed Mother told Estelle that everybody who wore the scapular would receive many graces from Jesus. Mary herself would bring Jesus' graces and dispense them as she wishes since Jesus does not deny her anything.

On their final meeting, Our Lady told Estelle to present the scapular to the bishop to help propagate this devotion. Estelle took the message to the Archbishop of Bourges who immediately established the devotion under the title of "Mother of Mercy" or "Our Lady of Pellevoisin" in 1894.[29]

---

[29] "Pellevoisin (France) 1876. Foundation Mary Pages." (https://www.marypages.com/pellevoisin-france-en.html). September 27, 2018.

Our Lady of Soufanieh

In December 1982, Our Lady appeared in **Damascus, Syria** to a girl named Mary Kourbet Al-Akhras.

Mary described the apparition Our Lady by stating that a globe of light appears and opens up and the Virgin Mary appears. Our Lady was dressed in white with a blue belt, a veil that covered her head, and a blue scarf that went over her shoulder. On her right hand, she held a Rosary that was made of crystal while her left arm was down by her side.

On the first visit, Mary ran away frightened when she saw the Virgin Mary. On the second, the Virgin Mary tells her to love and show love and compassion for everybody.

She also tells Mary to pray because the time of great tribulation will come and we will need to be close to God. Our Lady also tells Mary that to preach about Jesus and that she will help pour out graces to anyone who prays, even if people are weak in their prayers. Our Lady also gave her a prayer to recite which was, "God saves me, Jesus enlightens me, the Holy Spirit is my life, thus I fear nothing."

On another apparition, Our Lady was crying but smiled at Mary and then disappeared. On her fifth and last apparition, Our Lady tells them that she would like a shrine, not a church, to be built in that area. She told Mary to always pray and reflect on the Annunciation how she herself was God's servant and so she herself

---

"Our Lady of Pellevoisin, France." *Our Lady of Pellevoisin*. Roman Catholic Saints. (https://www.roman-catholic-saints.com/our-lady-of-pellevoisin.html). September 27, 2018.

Carpenter, John. "Our Lady of Pellevoisin, France, 1876." *Marian Apparitions*. Divine Mysteries and Miracles. July 28, 2016. (http://www.divinemysteries.info/our-lady-of-pellevoisin-france-1876/). September 27, 2018.

Ewing, Jeannie. "This is the Most Complete List of Marian Apparitions." The Mystical Humanity of Christ Publishing. (https://www.coraevans.com/blog/article/this-is-the-most-complete-list-of-marian-apparitions). September 27, 2018.

should also imitate her in that state.

Today, the site where the Virgin Mary appeared in is a place of worship where people have prayed in every day since November 1982. The prayers that are mainly prayed are the Rosary and other common prayers. [30]

---

[30] "Our Lady of Soufanieh, Damascus, Syria: Source of the Holy Oil." *Unity of Hearts – Unity of Christians, Unification of the Date of the Feast of Easter*. February 2, 2018. (http://soufanieh.com/menuenglish.htm). September 28, 2018.

Our Lady of Walsingham

On 1061 in the village of Walsingham in Norfolk, England, Our Lady appeared to Richeldis de Faverches.

The Virgin Mary showed Richeldis the house where the Annunciation occurred. She asked Richeldis that she would like a shrine that looked exactly like her house did back where she received the message from St. Gabriel the Archangel.

Our Lady promised Richeldis that she would grant refuge and graces to those who honored her in that shrine. Richeldis saw Our Lady three times and each time, Our Lady would give her instructions, such as the architectural measurements etc. Richeldis and the carpenters tried to build the shrine but did not know where to build it or how.

After a long night of prayer, Richeldis heard angelic singing coming from the direction of the shrine. Richeldis went out to investigate and discovered that the shrine had been moved a few yards away and was completed. Then she saw angels ascending back to Heaven while still singing.

The shrine was completed in 1053.

By the early 1500s, the shrine of Our Lady of Walsingham became a very popular pilgrimage area where many people traveled. However, in 1538, the Protestant bishop, Latimer, condemned the shrine as a trick from the devil and King Henry VIII ordered the shrine destroyed.

In the year of 1897, Pope Leo XIII ordered the restoration of the shrine.

Today, the shrine is the center of the National Shrine of Our Lady of Walsingham. [31]

---

[31] Marshall, Dr. Taylor. "England's Marian Apparition: Our Lady of Walsingham." Taylor Marshall Ph.D.: Stay Salty my Friends. (https://taylormarshall.com/2012/02/englands-marian-apparition-our-lady-of.html). September 30, 2018.

Reconciler of Nations

In March 1976, Our Lady appeared to Maria Esperanza in Cua, Venezuela.

In this apparition, Our Lady introduced herself as the "Reconciler of Nations."

Our Lady showed Maria her hands and told her that her hands were filled with graces and covered in splendor.

She told her that the purpose of her visit was to convert her children and to reconcile all the nations to herself.

Upon hearing about the apparition, many people visited the site and made it an unofficial site for prayer.

On March 1948, around 150 people gathered at the site and had Mass there.

When Mass was over, the people started going home.

However, some children were playing by a waterfall when they saw the Virgin Mary smiling at them.

They spoke about the apparition and urged the people to follow them.

The group of people who visited also saw the Virgin Mary and baby Jesus.

The apparitions lasted for intervals of about five to ten minutes and then half an hour at dusk.

Since the apparitions began, many people claimed that that location was always filled with an abundant number of flowers; they would hear beautiful music from an invisible choir, beautiful lights, movements of the sun, and many other miracles.

After the group of people saw the apparition of Our Lady, the church decided to investigate them.

The local bishop, Most Reverend Pio Bello Ricardo, performed an investigation and after three years, he claimed that the apparitions were in fact supernatural.

The bishop also declared the site as a "sacred ground" and thus made it a sacred site meant for prayer and reflection.

32

---

[32] "Betania, Venezuela: Apparitions, Healings, and the Mystic Maria Esperanza." The Catholic Travel Guide. (https://thecatholictravelguide.com/destinations/venezuela/betania-venezuela-apparitions-healings-mystic-maria-esperanza/). September 28, 2018.

"Virgen de Betania." Tradicion y Cultura. Venezuelatuya.com. (https://venezuelatuya.com/religion/betania.htm). September 28, 2018.

Policarpio, Arthur. "The Betania Apparitions of the Blessed Virgin Mary." *Totus Tuus, Maria!* (http://www.all-about-the-virgin-mary.com/betania-apparitions.html). September 28, 2018.

Our Lady of Eternal Aid

On August 1652, Our Lady appeared to Jeanne Courtel Querrien, Bretania, France.

Jeanne Courtel had been born deaf and mute but despite this, she still prayed and loved God.

One day, while she was watching her father's sheep, Our Lady appeared to her and asked her for a sheep.

The apparition began when Jeanne was praying.

A sudden gust of wind blew towards her and a bright light revealed the Virgin Mary.

The Virgin Mary was dressed in a bright white dress and golden halo. She was holding Baby Jesus in her arms.

Jeanne told her that they were her father's sheep but if she wanted, she would ask her father for permission.

The Virgin Mary smiled and waited as Jeanne ran to her father.

When Jeanne told her father, her father was amazed to hear her speak so he was willing to give Our Lady their entire flock.

Jeanne saw many visions of Our Lady where the Blessed Virgin told Jeanne that she would like a chapel to be built in her honor.

The Virgin Mary told Jeanne to find a statue that had been sculpted by St. Gall.

St. Gall had sculpted the statue in the year 610 A.D. and erected a pilgrimage there.

However, the shrine had been destroyed over time and the statue got lost.

Therefore, as a sign of her apparition, the Virgin Mary told

Jeanne to find it and present it to the bishop.

Jeanne did as the Holy Virgin had requested and presented the Bishop of Saint-Brieus, the Archbishop Denis de La Barde.

After an investigation, the bishop approved the apparitions and construction of the chapel began on September 1652.

Since then, many pilgrims had visited the site and in 1950, Britain's bishops coroneted the statue of Our Lady of All Help.

33

---

[33] *"Our Lady of Eternal Aid."* Querrien, Bretania, France (1652). *Marian Apparitions.* (http://www.miraclehunter.com/marian_apparitions/approved_apparitions/querrien/index.html). October 1, 2018.

Carpenter, John. "Our Lady of Eternal Aid, Querrin, France, 1652." *Marian Apparitions*. Divine Mysteries and Miracles. (http://www.divinemysteries.info/our-lady-of-eternal-aid-querrien-france-1652/). October 1, 2018.

Our Lady of Good Help

On October of 1859, the Virgin Mary appeared Champion, Wisconsin to a young Belgian immigrant woman, Adele Brise.

The Blessed Mother identified herself as "the Queen of Heaven who prays for the conversion of sinners."

The Virgin Mary was dressed in a dazzling white dress that fell to her feet and a yellow sash around her waist.

She also had a crown of stars on her head and golden hair that reached her shoulders.

She asked Adele to do the same and to teach people how to pray and get closer to God.

The Virgin Mary told Adele to try to convert sinners and do penance so that God wouldn't have to punish them.

Our Lady told Adele to go to confession daily and receive Holy Communion as reparation.

Shortly after, a chapel was built there in honor of Our Lady of Good Help.

[34]

---

[34] *"Our Lady of Good Help."* Robinsonville (now Champion), WI, USA (1859). The Miracle Hunter. (http://www.marianapparitions.org/marian_apparitions/approved_apparitions/robinsonville/index.html). October 1, 2018.

Sly, Randy. "Wisconsin Shrine Approved as First U.S. Marian Apparition Site." Catholic Online. December 11, 2010. (https://www.catholic.org/news/hf/faith/story.php?id=39511). October 1, 2018.

Our Lady of Good Success

On 1594, Our Lady appeared to Mother Mariana de Jesus Torres at her convent in Quito, Ecuador.

Mother Mariana had died in 1582 and after visiting Heaven, she chose to return to earth and lead a life of suffering as expiation for the sins that were going to be committed on the 20th century.

She died again in 1588 and after seeing terrible sins and abuses that were going to happen in the church, she chose to come back.

On 1594, Our Lady finally appeared to Mother Mariana and asked her to create a statue of her in her likeness.

Mother Mariana chose Francisco del Castillo to sculpt the statue.

When Francisco ran out of paint, Our Lady appeared with St. Francis and the Archangels: St. Michael, St. Gabriel, and St. Raphael to finish the statue.

The three Archangels bowed down in front of the Blessed Mother and praised her by singing.

St. Michael sang, "'Hail to Thee, Mary Most Holy Daughter of God the Father.'" (The Miracle Hunter, no. pag.)

St. Gabriel sang, "'Hail to Thee, Mary Most Holy Mother of God the Son.'" (The Miracle Hunter, no. pag.)

St. Raphael sang, "'Hail to Thee, Mary Most Holy, Most Pure Spouse of the Holy Ghost.'" (The Miracle Hunter, no. pag.)

Then the three Archangels together sang, "'Hail to Thee, Mary Most Holy Temple and Sacrarium of the Most Holy Trinity.'" (The Miracle Hunter, no. pag.)

When they finished the statue, the statue became animated as the Virgin Mary entered the statue.

Our Lady began to sing the "Magnificat" while the angels began to sing the "Salve Sancta Parens."

The rest of the nuns heard the singing and rushed into the church.

They found the statue transformed and surrounded by bright heavenly light.

The statue was placed above the seat of the Abbess and is officially blessed by the bishop.

[35]

---

[35] "Quito, Ecuador (1594)." Bishop Approved Apparitions. The Miracle Hunter. (http://www.marianapparitions.org/marian_apparitions/approved_apparitions/bishop.html). October 1, 2018.

To be continued…

Made in the USA
Coppell, TX
28 October 2022